A CRY IN THE DARK

Sound and the science of survival

Richard and Louise Spilsbury

WATTS

First published in 2014 by
Franklin Watts
338 Euston Road
London NW1 3BH

Franklin Watts Australia
Level 17/207 Kent Street
Sydney NSW 2000

Produced for Franklin Watts by
White-Thomson Publishing
+44 (0)843 208 7460
www.wtpub.co.uk

Series concept and editor: Alice Harman
Series consultant: Penny Coltman
Designer: Alix Wood
Experiment and character artworks: Stefan Chabluk

A CIP catalogue record for this book is available from
the British Library.

HB ISBN: 978 1 4451 2299 1
Library ebook ISBN: 978 1 4451 2591 6
Dewey Classification: 534

Picture Credits
Shutterstock: Africa Studio, angelo gilardelli, Axel Wolf, AXL, Dja65, grekoff, Horiyan, Hxdbzxy, jeka84, JIANG HONGYAN, Jonathan Lenz, LanKS, LehaKoK, Mark Yuill, Marko Poplasen, Matthew Cole, Mrs_ya, Oliver Sved, patpitchaya, Paul Fleet, phildaint, pzAxe, R. Gino Santa Maria, Sergey Chirkov, Sergey Novikov, Theeraphat, Tomislav Pinter, Wicek Listwan Fotografie, YorkBerlin.

Every attempt has been made to clear copyright. Should there be any inadvertent omissions, please apply to the publisher for rectification.

Printed in China

Franklin Watts is a division of Hachette Children's Books, an Hachette UK Company.

www.hachette.co.uk

Bold words in the text are included in the glossary

WHO'S WHO?

JESS

Jess is a bit of a daredevil. She's always first to try something new. She loves skateboarding, climbing and adventure stories.

BEN

Ben is a bit of a kit monster. He carries his rucksack with him at all times and it's full of useful – and not so useful – stuff.

AMELIE

Amelie is a science whizz. She's not a know-it-all, but she often has the right answers. She isn't too keen on getting her clothes dirty and her hair messed up.

ZAC

Zac is the youngest and although he never wants to be left out, he can get a bit nervous and is easily spooked.

CONTENTS

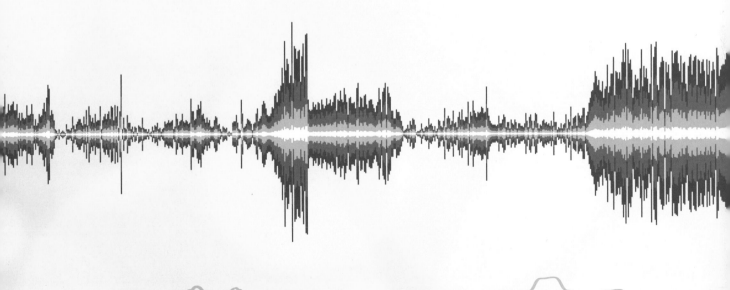

STRANGE SOUNDS

'Wait, you lot! Amelie's dad told us to stay here. We shouldn't go off on our own,' cries Zac. 'Look, Jess, there are snacks here!'

'Mmm, tempting,' says Jess. 'But we have to investigate those weird cries. Someone could be in trouble.'

'Yeah, or a mad scientist might have sneaked into the **technology park** after hours to do secret experiments!' suggests Ben gleefully.

'It's okay, Zac – my dad was going to give us a tour later. We're just doing it a bit sooner, that's all...' says Amelie slyly. 'Anyway, I'm intrigued now. I have to work out who or what made those strange noises. Let's go!'

WHAT DO YOU THINK?

How do different things make different sounds?

PROVE IT!

Investigate making sounds with different **materials**.
You need:

- large objects such as a cardboard box, a wooden board, a plastic tray and a tin
- pencil
- paintbrush
- metal spoon
- empty plastic containers with lids
- small objects such as beads, coins, paper clips, rubber bands and erasers

1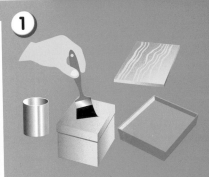

First line up your large objects on a flat surface. Do any of them make a sound when they are still? Tap and scratch the objects with the pencil, paintbrush and metal spoon. Does this create any sounds? If so, are the sounds different to each other?

2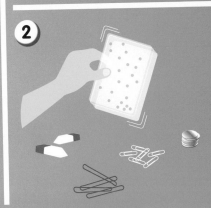

Put one type of small object inside a container and close the lid tightly. Shake the container and listen. Try the same thing with the other small objects. What kinds of sound do they make?

WHY IT WORKS

Different types of materials and objects can make a variety of different sounds. However, they don't make sounds when they are still. In order for materials or objects to make sounds, we need to make them move by striking, plucking, blowing or shaking them. We hear the sounds made because they travel from their **source** to our ears.

WHERE ARE WE?

'Sorry...' sighs Jess, as they arrive in an empty **laboratory** at the end of a long corridor. 'I thought I heard the sound coming from this **direction**.'

'The only thing coming from this direction is the nasty, nostril-stinging stench of that green gloop!' exclaims Zac, pointing to a strange, glowing substance.

'Maybe my mad scientist theory was spot on,' says Ben. 'Something's definitely not right here.'

'The only thing that's not right here is us following Jess on a wild goose chase!' snaps Amelie. 'She's got an ear bud in one ear, listening to music. You need both ears to work out where a sound is coming from.'

WHAT DO YOU THINK?

Is Amelie right? Can you hear sounds better if you use two ears rather than one?

PROVE IT!

Test how our ears help us sense the direction that a sound comes from.

You need:

- five friends ● five small pots with lids
- dry (uncooked) lentils or rice ● scarf ● chair

1 Make five shakers by putting a few dry rice grains or lentils into each pot and putting the lids on tightly.

2 Tie the scarf over your eyes and sit on the chair. Your friends should stand in a circle around you, about a metre away. They take it in turns to rattle their shakers very softly, so you can just hear them. Can you point to who makes the sound each time?

3 Do the same again, but this time cover one of your ears so you can only hear sounds in one ear. What happens? Swap places and let your friends take turns on the chair.

WHY IT WORKS

Sounds don't travel in just one direction from their source. They spread out all around in **sound waves**, like ripples in a pond when you throw in a stone. It's easier to judge exactly where a sound comes from by using two ears, because the ear closest to the sound hears it a little louder and slightly sooner than the other ear.

SETTING TRAPS

'Come on, let's not argue,' says Ben. 'We can find out if anyone's around by setting traps. If we balance these metal trays from the laboratory on top of the doors, they'll fall off and make a noise if someone opens a door.'

'Am I the only sane person here?' cries Zac. 'If a mad scientist is roaming about, shouldn't we be heading in the opposite direction?'

'Stop whining and grab a tray, Zac,' says Jess. 'It's a great idea.'

'Maybe not,' says Amelie. 'I just dropped a tray and it didn't make much of a sound.'

'That's because it dropped on a mat and didn't **vibrate**,' says Ben. 'Sounds are caused by vibrations – I thought you'd know that, Amelie!'

PROVE IT!

Test the idea that vibrations make sound.
You need:

● friend ● balloon

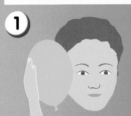

1 Blow up the balloon as big as you can, but be careful not to pop it. Tie the end tightly so that no air can escape. Hold the balloon against one of your ears.

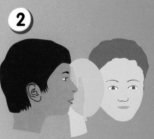

2 Ask your friend to press their lips against the other side of the balloon and speak into it. What happens? Try the same thing again, but this time you speak and your friend listens.

WHY IT WORKS

Sound is produced when things vibrate. When something vibrates, it repeatedly moves up and down, or backwards and forwards, very quickly. Air vibrates in our throat when we speak. When vibrations leave our mouths and hit other things, they make those other things vibrate too. When you speak into the balloon, you can feel the sounds you are making as the balloon's skin vibrates against your lips. When you hold the balloon to your ear, you can hear and feel sound vibrations through the balloon.

DANGER WITHIN

'The sound traps worked!' cries Ben triumphantly. 'Someone or something made one of the trays fall off a door near here. Maybe they went into this laboratory...'

'Well, we can't just barge in if it is a mad scientist. That'll only make him madder!' says Jess. 'And if we try to look in, he'll see us in this bright light.'

'We need a way of listening to what's going on in there,' says Zac.

'That's it, Zac!' says Amelie. 'We'll make an **ear trumpet** to hear whether anyone is inside.'

'I'm glad I thought of it!' says Zac, grinning proudly. 'But what's an ear trumpet?'

'It's a device to help us hear better. If we hold the wide end against the wall, we should be able to hear what's going on inside that room,' explains Amelie.

WHAT DO YOU THINK?

Is Amelie right? Can ear trumpets help us hear better?

PROVE IT!

Make and test an ear trumpet to see if it works. You need:

● A4 sheet of card ● scissors ● sticky tape

1 Roll the sheet of card into a **cone** shape, and tape it so the edges don't come apart. This is your ear trumpet.

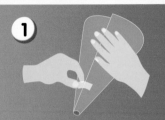

WHY IT WORKS

You should hear better with the ear trumpet. The cone shape collects sound waves together and **funnels** them into the ear, instead of them spreading out in all directions. The bigger the wide end of the ear trumpet, the more sound waves it gathers. The narrower the end of the cone you hold to your ear, the more the sound waves are focused. This is like the way your **outer ear** collects sound waves and funnels them into the **inner ear** to help you hear sounds.

2 Listen to a sound coming from a nearby radio or speaker without the ear trumpet. Now listen to the same sound with the ear trumpet held gently to one ear (cover your other ear to strengthen the effect). What do you notice?

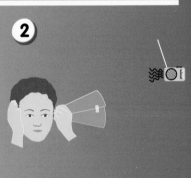

ON THE RUN

'Well, your mad scientist isn't in that lab, so where is he now?' asks Jess.

'I think we're about to find out,' answers Ben. 'The weird wailing sound is getting louder, which must mean he's getting closer.'

'Well, what are we waiting for? Run!' shouts Zac, sprinting off with Jess and Amelie close behind him.

'Nooo!' shouts Jess suddenly, as she overtakes Zac and runs smack into a huge, locked metal door. 'This is a dead end.'

'There's no way out,' shouts Zac. 'We're cornered!'

'Don't panic,' says Ben, panting as he catches up with the rest. 'I think the sound is getting quieter. He must be heading away from us again.'

'Are you sure?' trembles Amelie.

WHAT DO YOU THINK?

Is Ben right? Are sounds quieter if their sources are further away from us?

PROVE IT!

Test whether sounds are quieter as they get further away from us

You need:

● friends ● tape measure ● chalk ● bunch of keys

1 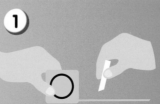 Use the tape measure and chalk to mark 5-metre **distances** on a straight 25-metre path, from a fixed starting point.

2 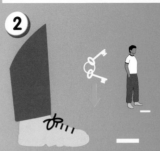 Stand at the starting point and ask your friend to start at the first 5-metre mark. Your friend listens as you drop the keys, and tells you how loud a sound the keys make when they hit the ground.

3  Ask your friend to stand at each distance mark in turn, moving further away from you. Each time he or she is at a further distance mark, drop the keys and ask whether the sound is louder, softer or the same as at the last mark. Note down the responses. Try the test with several different friends.

WHY IT WORKS

Ben is right. Your friends should notice that the further away the keys are, the quieter the sound is when they are dropped. Sound uses up **energy** as it moves, which means that the sound seems quieter when the source of the sound (the dropped keys) moves further away. Loud sounds have more energy, so they travel further from their source. Quiet sounds have less energy, so you have to be closer to hear them.

BEN BECOMES BAIT

'It's time to stop running and find out who or what this thing is once and for all,' says Ben. 'If one of us makes a noise and lures him into the boiler room, the others can trap him.'

'There's no way I'm doing that!' says Zac, quickly. 'It's your bright idea, Ben – you can be the bait.'

'Okay, you big chicken,' sighs Ben. 'But how can we make sounds loud enough to be heard through all those long corridors?'

'We need to find something really big to make loud sounds,' says Jess. 'Look, there's a huge metal cover in there – Ben can hit that with the piece of broken pipe lying on the floor.'

'Brilliant! Although we don't necessarily need a big object to make a loud noise,' says Amelie. 'Bigger vibrations make louder sounds, so hitting a smaller thing very hard will also make lots of noise.'

EERIE ECHOES

'Well, your mad scientist wasn't loopy enough to fall for your trap, Ben!' laughs Amelie, as the four friends walk along an empty, high-walled corridor.

'No, obviously not – and now my ears are ringing because I banged that big cover so hard,' says Ben crossly.

'Shush for a minute,' says Jess. 'I think I hear footsteps behind us.'

'Now who's getting spooked?' teases Zac. 'I thought I was supposed to be the chicken!'

'I'm serious,' snaps Jess. 'I can hear other footsteps besides our own. Listen.'

'It's just an **echo**,' says Amelie. 'At least, I hope that's all it is...'

**WHAT DO
YOU THINK?**

Is Amelie right? Are the sounds
likely to be echoes in a corridor
with flat, hard surfaces?

PROVE IT!

Test how echoes work.
You need:

● two long cardboard tubes (from kitchen rolls
or wrapping paper rolls)
● metal tray ● masking tape ● ticking clock
● 30 cm ruler ● table

1  Tape the tubes to a table to
make a wide V-shape, with
the ends of the tubes close but
not touching. Put the ticking
clock just by the end of one
tube, at the wide end of the
V-shape. Cover one ear and
press your other ear to the end
of the other tube. What can
you hear?

2  Now tape the metal tray to the
edge of the table. It needs to
be placed on its side, near to
where the two tubes almost
meet. Listen again. What can
you hear? Try adjusting the
angle of the tubes a little if you
don't hear anything.

WHY IT WORKS

The first time you listened, you probably didn't hear
the ticking. But when the tray is in place, the sound
bounces off it and comes up the other tube so you can
hear the clock. An echo like this happens when sound
reflects off the surface of an object and travels back
away from it again. Hard surfaces reflect sound better
than soft surfaces. If you still can't hear the ticking
clock with the metal tray in place, changing the angle
your tube makes with the tray should help.

LYING IN WAIT

'Right, I've got a plan to find out if someone is following us,' says Ben.

'Not another one of your nutty plans!' says Zac. 'If we go along with it, will you promise we can go back afterwards?'

'Let's hear it first,' says Jess.

'Well, we split into two teams and watch both corridors at the same time,' says Ben. 'It's a classic **stakeout**.'

'You've been watching too many detective films!' says Amelie. 'And how will we contact each other without the mad scientist hearing us?'

'We'll use plastic cups and string from my rucksack to make a telephone,' replies Ben. 'As long as the string is stretched out straight and **taut**, it will work.'

'What?' exclaims Zac. 'I'll believe that works when I see it – or hear it, rather.'

WHAT DO YOU THINK?

Is Ben right? Can sound travel through string?

PROVE IT!

Try making a string telephone.
You need:

- two plastic cups
- sharpened pencil
- long piece of string
- two paper clips
- friend

2 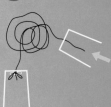 Tie the paper clip to one end of the string. Push the other end of the string into a cup and through the hole in the bottom. Thread the string through the hole in the other cup, from the outside to the inside. Tie the second paper clip to the end of the string, so it stops the end of the string slipping back out of that cup, too.

1 Use the pencil to carefully poke a small hole in the bottom of each plastic cup.

3  Pull the cups so that the string is stretched tight and not touching anything else. Your friend should talk quietly into one cup while you hold the other cup to your ear.

WHY IT WORKS

Ben is right. Sounds usually travel through the air to our ears, but sound can move through other materials, too. Sound travels better through some materials than others. Sound vibrations travel well through string, as long as you make sure that the string is straight, taut and not touching anything else. If it is touching something else, the string won't vibrate freely.

GOTCHA!

'The plan worked. Someone's coming!' whispers Zac into his telephone cup, as a strange wailing and scraping sound gets louder and closer to him.

'What is it?' cries Amelie in horror, as she and Ben run over. 'It doesn't sound human.'

'It's not!' shouts Jess, rushing down the corridor towards a dark, moving shape. 'It's a cat! The poor thing's tangled in some sort of mesh. We've got to take it back to Amelie's dad and get him to cut it free.'

'Not if it keeps wailing like that!' complains Zac as Jess walks back towards them, carrying the noisy cat.

'It's too scared to stop,' says Jess. 'We'll make ear muffs so you can't hear it – but what will block out that racket?'

PROVE IT!

Test how well different materials block out sounds.
You need:

● two plastic or polystyrene cups
● ticking clock or radio at a low **volume**
● different materials, such as cotton wool, shredded paper, tissue and bubble wrap

1 Put the ticking clock or the radio on a nearby surface, and place the empty plastic beakers over your ears. Listen to the clock or the radio. If you can't hear anything, move the clock or radio closer to you.

2 Now fill the plastic cups with one of the materials. Put the cups to your ears and listen to the ticking clock or the radio again. The clock or radio needs to be exactly as far away from you as before. What do you notice?

3 Test all of the other materials in the same way. Which material is best at blocking out the sounds?

WARNING:

Never put anything inside your ears. This can be very dangerous, and may permanently damage your hearing.

WHY IT WORKS

Some materials **absorb** sound better than others. Soft, bumpy materials such as fabric and rubber absorb sound best, so they make the best sound **insulators**. Hard, smooth surfaces reflect sound. That's why a room with carpets, soft seats and curtains sounds different to an empty room with a wooden floor.

MAKING MUSIC

'Dad!' cries Amelie, when they get back to the lab. 'Didn't you even notice we'd gone?'

'Gone? Did you go somewhere?' says Amelie's dad, looking up from his work.'

'Never mind,' sighs Amelie. 'Look, you need to cut the metal mesh off this cat we found.'

'How did that get in here? It must have got caught in a **ventilation shaft** on its way inside. This could take a while. Play some music to calm it down while I cut it free...'

'How can we make music?' asks Amelie. 'Ben has a lot of stuff in that huge rucksack of his, but even he doesn't carry around a selection of musical instruments!'

'Use some water and those **test tubes**, then,' Amelie's dad suggests.

WHAT DO YOU THINK?

Is Amelie's dad right? Can you use water in tubes to make music?

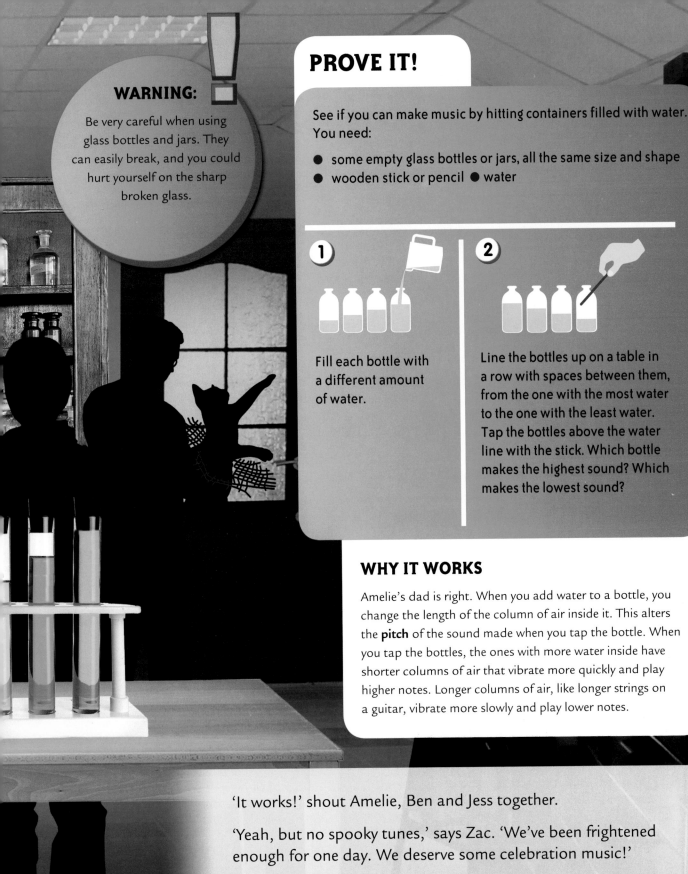

PROVE IT!

See if you can make music by hitting containers filled with water. You need:

- some empty glass bottles or jars, all the same size and shape
- wooden stick or pencil ● water

1

Fill each bottle with a different amount of water.

2

Line the bottles up on a table in a row with spaces between them, from the one with the most water to the one with the least water. Tap the bottles above the water line with the stick. Which bottle makes the highest sound? Which makes the lowest sound?

WHY IT WORKS

Amelie's dad is right. When you add water to a bottle, you change the length of the column of air inside it. This alters the **pitch** of the sound made when you tap the bottle. When you tap the bottles, the ones with more water inside have shorter columns of air that vibrate more quickly and play higher notes. Longer columns of air, like longer strings on a guitar, vibrate more slowly and play lower notes.

'It works!' shout Amelie, Ben and Jess together.

'Yeah, but no spooky tunes,' says Zac. 'We've been frightened enough for one day. We deserve some celebration music!'

QUIZ

1 **Which of these statements is false?**

a) Sounds spread out in all directions from their source.

b) Sounds are made when something vibrates.

c) Sounds can be made by things that are still.

2 **When you stop something – such as a rubber band or drum skin – from vibrating, what happens?**

a) The sound stops.

b) The sound gets louder.

c) The sound gets quieter.

4 **How does an ear trumpet help people to hear better?**

a) It makes them concentrate more on the sounds.

b) It collects and carries more sound waves to their ears.

c) It makes sounds travel further.

3 **Why do we have two ears?**

a) to keep sunglasses on our faces

b) because it's easier to judge where a sound comes from by using two ears

c) because if we didn't, we'd only hear half of the sounds around us

5 **Why do sounds get quieter the further away we are from them?**

a) We stop listening carefully when we cannot see the source so well.

b) Sounds lose energy as they travel, which means they are quieter by the time they reach our ears.

c) Quieter sounds don't make the air vibrate.

6

What is an echo?

a) a sound that gets louder

b) a sound that gets absorbed by a soft material

c) a sound that is repeated as the sound waves reflect off a hard surface

7

Which of these statements is true?

a) Sound can only travel through air.

b) Sound travels better through some materials than others.

c) Sound can only travel on Sundays.

8

What happens when you hit an object harder?

a) The pitch of the sound it makes gets higher.

b) The sound gets louder.

c) The pitch of the sound gets lower.

9

What is the pitch of a sound?

a) how high or low it is

b) how long it lasts

c) how loud it is

10

If you tap an empty glass bottle and listen to the sound, then put water into the bottle and tap it again, the sound is...

a) the same pitch as before

b) lower in pitch

c) higher in pitch

FIND OUT MORE

BOOKS

Bang! Sound and How We Hear Things (The Real Scientist)
Peter Riley, Franklin Watts, 2012

Ear-splitting Sounds and Other Vile Noises (Disgusting and Dreadful Science)
Anna Claybourne, Franklin Watts, 2013

Sound and Light (Hands-on Science)
Sarah Angliss, Kingfisher, 2013

Light and Sound (Essential Physical Science)
Louise & Richard Spilsbury, Raintree, 2014

Sound (Science Detective Investigates)
Harriet McGregor, Wayland, 2011

WEBSITES

Discover more about how our ears work:
www.childrensuniversity.manchester.ac.uk/interactives/science/brainandsenses/ear

Have a go at changing the sounds instruments make:
www.bbc.co.uk/schools/scienceclips/ages/9_10/changing_sounds.shtml

Find out more about sound and hearing:
www.fi.edu/fellows/fellow2/apr99/soundindex.html

Every effort has been made by the publisher to ensure that these websites contain no inappropriate or offensive material. However, because of the nature of the Internet, it is impossible to guarantee that the content of these sites will not be altered. We strongly advise that Internet access is supervised by a responsible adult.

GLOSSARY

absorb to take something in, for example a sponge absorbs water

cone shape that is round at the bottom and pointed at the top

direction way in which something or someone travels or faces

distance the space between places and/or objects

ear trumpet device that people in the past used to help them hear

echo sound that is repeated as sound waves reflect off a surface

energy power that makes things work, happen or move

funnel to narrow the flow of something

inner ear part of the ear that is inside the skull

insulator substance that does not easily allow sound (or heat or electrical energy) to move through it

laboratory a room where people do scientific experiments, often with special equipment

material type of substance, such as wood, cotton or plastic, from which things are made

outer ear part of the ear that is visible on the outside of the head

pitch how low (deep) or high (squeaky) a sound is

reflect to bend or throw back something, such as sound or light

sound wave vibration in the air that we hear as sound

source where something comes from

stakeout to watch a certain place or person, while staying hidden and quiet to avoid being seen or heard

taut stretched or pulled tight

technology park place where scientists carry out experiments and other types of research

test tubes thin, glass tubes that are used to hold materials in science experiments

ventilation shaft passage that brings fresh air into a building

vibrate to move forwards and backwards or up and down very quickly, again and again

volume how loud a sound is

INDEX